D1294552

Celebrating Differences

Different Abilities

by Rebecca Pettiford

Bullfrog Books

Ideas for Parents and Teachers

Bullfrog Books let children practice reading informational text at the earliest reading levels. Repetition, familiar words, and photo labels support early readers.

Before Reading

- Discuss the cover photo. What does it tell them?

- Look at the picture glossary together. Read and discuss the words.

Read the Book

- "Walk" through the book and look at the photos. Let the child ask questions. Point out the photo labels.

- Read the book to the child, or have him or her read independently.

After Reading

- Prompt the child to think more. Ask: What special abilities do you have?

Bullfrog Books are published by Jump!
5357 Penn Avenue South
Minneapolis, MN 55419
www.jumplibrary.com

Library of Congress Cataloging-in-Publication Data

Names: Pettiford, Rebecca, author.
Title: Different abilities / by Rebecca Pettiford.
Description: Minneapolis, MN: Jump!, Inc., [2017]
Series: Celebrating differences | Audience: Age 5–8.
Audience: Grade Pre-school, excluding K.
Includes bibliographical references and index.
Identifiers: LCCN 2016056349 (print)
LCCN 2017006779 (ebook) | ISBN 9781620316672
(hardcover: alk. paper) | ISBN 9781620317204 (pbk.)
ISBN 9781624965449 (ebook)
Subjects: LCSH:
People with disabilities—Juvenile literature.
Classification: LCC HV1568 .P48 2017 (print)
LCC HV1568 (ebook) | DDC 362.4—dc23
LC record available at https://lccn.loc.gov/2016056349

Editor: Jenny Fretland VanVoorst
Book Designer: Leah Sanders
Photo Researcher: Leah Sanders

Photo Credits: Dreamstime: Stainedglass, 4.
Getty: Huntstock, 12, 14–15; Dorling Kindersley,
13; BRIAN MITCHELL, 20–21. iStock: FatCamera,
cover; baranozdemir, 1; andresr, 3. Shutterstock:
Haslam Photography, cover; karelnoppe, 8–9;
wavebreakmedia, 10–11; Jaren Jai Wicklund, 18–19;
Littlekidmoment, 22; Denis Kuvaev, 24. SuperStock:
Stockbyte, 5; Phanie, 6–7; Compassionate Eye
Foundation/Jetta Productions, 16, 17.

Printed in the United States of America at
Corporate Graphics in North Mankato, Minnesota.

Table of Contents

What Can You Do?

Everyone has special abilities.

Meg reads with her fingers.

How?

braille

Her book is in braille!

Tony plays the violin.

He practices every day.

Someday he may
be famous!

Allie is the fastest
girl at school.

Wheels spin faster
than legs run.

Want to race?

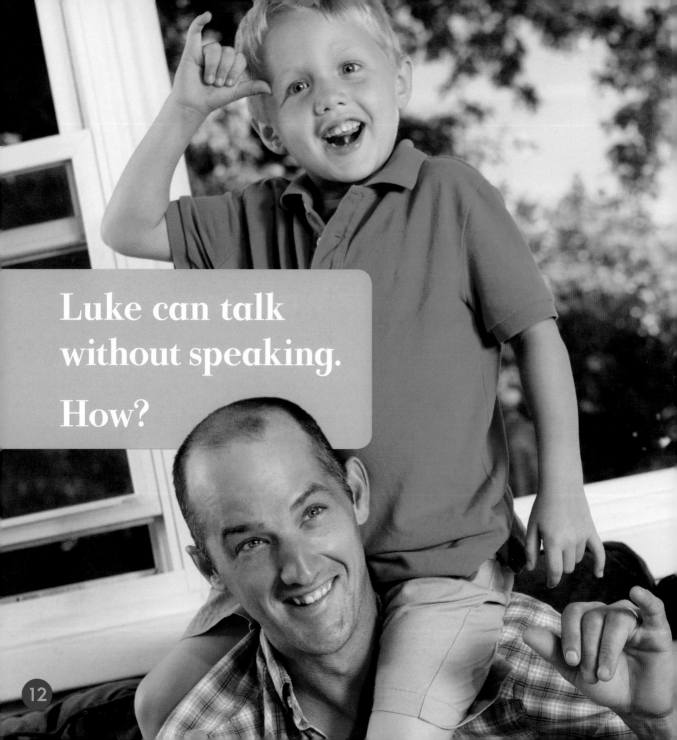

Luke can talk without speaking.

How?

12

He uses his hands.

When he talks
to Sam, no one
can hear them!

Cam is good with animals.
He loves his dog, Fig.

Fig is his service dog.
She keeps him safe.

Tou is great at checkers.
He beats all his friends.
He beats his mom, too!

What can you do?

Sign Language

Try learning a few words of American sign language. You'll be amazed by what you can say with your hands!

Picture Glossary

abilities
Natural or learned skills at doing something.

famous
Very well-known.

braille
A writing system used by blind people in which raised dots stand for letters.

service dog
A dog who is specially trained to help people with disabilities.

Index

To Learn More

Learning more is as easy as 1, 2, 3.

1) Go to www.factsurfer.com

2) Enter "differentabilities" into the search box.

3) Click the "Surf" button to see a list of websites.

With factsurfer.com, finding more information is just a click away.